Contents

Introduction 2

Chapter 1. What are gaps? 6

    What are Gaps Exactly? 10

    Why Do Gaps Matter? 15

    Why Do Gaps Form? The Psychology Behind Gaps And Impacts On the Market 18

    Implications of Gaps 24

    How To Identify Gaps Visually On Charts 26

    How To Differentiate True Gaps From Wicks (False Gaps) ... 30

Chapter 2: The different types of gaps Illustrated 36

    Illustration Of The Different Types Of Gap 37

    How Gaps Are Classified 39

    Common Types of Gaps 44

Chapter 3: Gap Trading Strategies 64

    Professional GAP Trading Strategy 80

Chapter 4: Risk management for trading gaps 105

    Market Volatility and Gap Trading: 107

    Position sizing analysis 111

    Emotion Management 117

    Backtesting and Review 122

Introduction

Gap trading is a captivating strategy that piqued my interest from the moment I heard about it from a fellow trader. Initially, I was skeptical about its actual profitability. I mean this is stock trading – every day, someone somewhere seems to be coming up with a new strategy for making "huge" profits from the market.

I always say if you want to try all the different trading strategies, techniques, and systems you hear about in trading, you will spend the rest of your life trying unique systems every day and end up making nothing at all.

To make money from stock trading, you need to adopt a winning strategy, actually master it, and then apply it without any emotional attachment. And this I have done for a long time, especially in my early days in the market.

With such a mantra, trying new techniques or systems was never my thing. But there was just something about gap trading that just sounded right to me. Something in the very idea of utilizing the "momentarily sharp up or downward movement" of stocks seems so intriguing that it makes me want to abandon everything I knew for the wild ride in the storm.

It's been five years since then and boy, am I glad that I made that sudden leap for gap trading. well, it's not exactly a sudden leap. the journey has not been all jolly good but as I delved deeper into gap trading, I discovered its potential.

My journey involved researching and analyzing various stocks and seeking exploitable gaps in the markets. Admittedly, it wasn't smooth sailing—I stumbled and learned from my fair share of mistakes. However, with time and experience, I honed my own gap trading strategy.

As my success in gap trading grew, I began sharing my insights with fellow traders. Many expressed interest in learning this strategy but lacked a starting point. That's when I decided to pen this book. My aim? To offer a comprehensive guide to gap trading, spanning from the fundamentals to advanced techniques. I want others to benefit from my triumphs and pitfalls, ultimately crafting their successful gap-trading approaches.

Within these pages, we'll explore everything you need to know about gap trading. We'll kick off with the basics: understanding what gaps and the dynamics behind this simple yet profitable concept, how gaps should function (– *theoretically*) how they *behave*, and why it can be a lucrative endeavor.

Next, we'll go deeper into the various types of gaps—breakaway, runaway, and exhaustion gaps—and learn how to spot and interpret them. Our journey will also encompass different gap trading strategies that I have learned over the years, some real examples of some of my most profitable gap trading strategies, and how you can make them yours.

As we progress, we'll venture into more advanced techniques. Imagine using options to trade gaps or integrating fundamental analysis into your gap trading strategy. We'll also discuss adapting your approach to different market conditions, whether bullish or bearish, range-bound, or volatile. And finally, we'll explore even more real-world examples and practical tips to enhance your gap trading prowess. ☑🔍

Chapter 1. What are gaps?

During my time with most stock traders, I found that using illustrations is one of the easiest ways to explain most concepts.

As such, I tend to use them a lot to convey my ideas and I find that such ideas tend to stick more when they are properly illustrated especially with a story. Everyone loves a good story and the more detailed and elaborate a story is, the more we tend to remember what they represent.

So, let's start this chapter of what gaps are with a very simple illustrative story. Remember the story is merely for illustrative purposes.

The story:

Imagine you're visiting a flea market known for its antique treasures. You stumble upon a stall selling vintage cameras, and you spot a classic film camera you've been wanting for ages.

Here's how the situation could unfold:

Scenario 1: The "Gap Up" and Filling the Gap:

1. **The Gap Up** You arrive at the flea market early and see the camera priced at a very reasonable $50. However, the seller informs you he received several calls about the camera and might raise the price later in the day. He closes his stall for a few hours.

2. **Returning to the Market:** When you return in the afternoon, the seller excitedly reveals he's been bombarded with inquiries and has raised the price to $100! This sudden jump in price, with no sales in between, creates a "gap up" on the imaginary price chart of the camera.

3. **Filling the Gap:** *You remember seeing the camera earlier at $50. You believe the price might eventually "fill the gap" and come back down to a more reasonable price. You decide to wait and see what happens.*

4. **Making the Purchase:** *Later in the day, with several potential buyers hesitant about the new price, the seller starts negotiating. You managed to buy the camera for $70, still a good deal but not as low as the initial $50.*

Scenario 2: Riding the Gap Up:

1. **The Gap Up** *You see the camera priced at $50 and, impressed with its condition, decide to buy it immediately. You're aware of the seller's earlier remarks about potential price hikes and believe the gap-up might be a sign of increasing demand.*

2. **Riding the Wave:** *Later in the day, the seller confirms your suspicion. He mentions selling several cameras at the new, higher price. You feel confident in your decision, knowing the price might continue to rise due to increased interest.*

3. **Potential Future Profit:** *You decide to hold onto the camera, hoping its value continues to climb. In the future, you might be able to sell it for an even higher price, profiting from the initial gap.*

These scenarios illustrate two ways to potentially profit from gap trading. In the first, you aim to **"fill the gap"** by buying after a price jump, hoping the price will eventually return to its previous level. In the second, you **"ride the gap up"** by buying during the jump, believing the price will continue to rise in the same direction.

It's important to remember that gap trading involves risks, and there's no guarantee the price will move in the way you anticipate. But I think you already are aware of such risks as a trader but if you are not, then I'm glad to inform you that trading gaps can be a very risky trade.

However, by understanding the concept of gaps and analyzing the market context, you can develop strategies to navigate these price movements and potentially profit from them.

What are Gaps Exactly?

So, what are the gaps exactly?

A stock gap is an area discontinuity in a security's chart where its price either rises or falls from the previous day's close with no trading occurring in between.

That's a lot of grammar.

A stock gap is a gap – a space. It is a space created by the differences in prices between when a stock was trading and when it was not trading. A stock gap is like a mysterious door that suddenly appears on a price chart. Imagine you're walking through a forest, and out of nowhere, you stumble upon a space—a gap! Here's what it means:

During regular trading hours, the stock price moves up and down as people buy and sell. But sometimes, when the market is closed (like at night or on weekends), something big happens. This big thing that happens may be positive to the stock or it may be negative to the stock.

The Surprise: News or events (like earnings reports, company announcements, or economic data) can cause a flood of buyers or sellers. When the market reopens, the stock price jumps significantly higher or lower than where it closed the previous day. This significant change in price from where the stock is close to the new opening price is the gap!

Now keep in mind that we said, the "big event" that caused the sudden jump in the price of the stock might be favorable to the stock price or might be harming the stock price. Hence the stock price might reach the ceiling or dunk deep into the ground, to a significantly lower price.

Whichever happens, there is a gap. And you can mine this gap for your profit whenever you want as long as you are careful enough to exploit it at the right time.

Enough with the theories already. Let's take a look at a real-world chart to find a gap. I hope this will help you identify a gap whenever you see one next time.

Let's take a look at this chart of a gap:

In the above image, we see a very visual representation of what an actual gap will look like on the chart on any trading platform. This

represents an actual space, a jump in the price of stocks from an original point to a new price without showing any continuity.

Think of it like this: when you count numerically, you need to progress from 1 to 2 to 3 to 4 and then 5, 6, 7 ... in the case of a gap, you could jump from 1-5 or 5 to 9. And this is the beauty of the jumps, you could come in before the jumps, buy your stock after carefully weighing your options, and then resell the stocks at the new warped price.

Stocks that jump up higher than their previous trading prices are said to be experiencing a 'Gap up' in their prices.

Gaps are not always progressive – they could regress as well. For instance, a stock trading before the market closes for the day at the rate of $5 could start trading on the next opening day at $1!

This is a 'Gap down'.

The space between the old price of the stock and the new trading price whether the stock gaps up or down gives the actual gap. These gaps sometimes may persist for a while in the market but as more and more traders buy and sell stocks, they start to level and settle into a more comfortable price.

This change provides a continuity that allows the gap to be filled. This is called the 'gap fill' and the gap fill happens when the stock price retraces its steps and moves up and down slowly to meet the demand until it balances out and becomes neutral again.

Stocks rarely stay neutral since they tend to move up and down by little points with every trade from around the globe.

Why Do Gaps Matter?

Gaps in stock trading matter because they can signal significant changes in the supply and demand for a particular stock, which can create opportunities for traders to profit. Here are some reasons why gaps matter in stock trading, along with examples to illustrate each point:

Gaps can indicate a change in market sentiment: Gaps can occur when there is a sudden shift in the way traders feel about a particular stock or the market as a whole. For example, if a company releases a positive earnings report after the market closes, it may cause a gap in the stock price when the market reopens. This gap-up indicates that traders are now more bullish on the stock, which can lead to further price increases.

Gaps can signal a change in the trend: Gaps can also indicate a change in the trend of a stock's price. For example, if a stock has been in a downtrend for several weeks but then gaps up, it may signal that the trend is reversing and the stock is now headed higher. Traders can use this information to adjust their strategies and take advantage of the new trend.

Gaps can create support and resistance levels: Gaps can create important support and resistance levels on a stock's chart. For example, if a stock gap is up, the top of the gap can act as a support level, as traders may be reluctant to sell below that price. Conversely, if a stock gaps down, the bottom of the gap can act as a resistance level, as traders may be hesitant to buy above that price.

Gaps can provide trading opportunities: Gaps can create trading opportunities for both short-term and long-term traders. For example, day traders may look to buy a stock that gaps up at the open and then sell it later in the day as the price continues to rise. Swing traders may look to buy a stock that gaps down and then hold it for several days or weeks, anticipating that the price will recover and fill the gap.

In summary, gaps in stock trading matter because they can indicate significant changes in market sentiment, signal a change in trend, create support and resistance levels, and provide trading opportunities for both short-term and long-term traders. By understanding how to interpret gaps and incorporate them into their strategies, traders can potentially increase their chances of success in the market.

Why Do Gaps Form? The Psychology Behind Gaps And Impacts On the Market

Gaps in stock trading form due to a significant disparity between supply and demand for a stock, leading to a price jump without any trades occurring between the jump. This disparity is often triggered by various factors that can influence the perception, valuation, or desire to own a stock.

There are many significant reasons why gaps form in the stock market. Understanding why gaps form the way they do and the timing is very important if you want to profit from your gap trading strategy. This is because most of the time you want to rely on these reasons to know when to buy into a gap, or not buy into it and when to exit the trade.

While I cannot give you an exhaustive list of the various reasons why gaps can happen in the charts, here are some of the most common ones and some that you might want to start paying attention to right away.

1. After-Hours News or Events

One of the most common reasons for gap formation is the release of news or events that affect a company's fundamentals or perceived value, occurring after the market has closed or before it opens. This includes:

- Earnings reports that surpass or fall short of expectations.
- Announcements of mergers, acquisitions, or divestitures.
- Changes in senior management or strategic direction.
- Regulatory updates or legal issues impacting operations.

Since the stock market is closed when this information is released, traders and investors must wait until the market opens to act on this news, resulting in a gap up or down from the previous close.

2. Market Sentiment

The collective mood or attitude of investors towards the market or a particular stock can lead to gap formation. This sentiment can shift rapidly due to:

- Economic indicators and forecasts, such as unemployment rates, inflation data, or consumer confidence indexes.
- Global events affecting international markets, like geopolitical tensions, elections, or significant policy changes by central banks.
- Industry-specific news impacting related stocks or the entire sector.

3. Technical Factors

Technical trading factors can also cause gaps, especially in stocks with high levels of speculative trading or when certain price levels are breached:

- Stop-loss orders getting triggered en masse, leading to a rapid decline or increase in stock price.

- Breakout or breakdown from a technical pattern, prompting a flurry of buying or selling activity.
- Liquidity gaps, especially in small-cap or thinly traded stocks, where the order book can't match buy and sell orders smoothly.

4. Psychological Factors

Investor psychology plays a significant role in gap formation. The decision-making process is influenced by:

- Fear and greed, driving overreactions to news or events.
- Herd behavior, where investors follow the majority, amplifying price movements.
- Confirmation bias, where investors give more weight to information that

confirms their existing beliefs, leading to exaggerated market reactions.

Implications of Gaps

Gaps in stock trading can have a significant impact on the market, affecting everything from stock prices to trading strategies. Here are some ways that gaps can impact the market:

Volatility: Gaps can cause increased volatility in the market as traders react to the news or event that caused the gap. This volatility can create opportunities for traders to profit from short-term price movements but can also increase risk.

Support and Resistance Levels: Gaps can create new support and resistance levels on a stock's chart. The top of a gap can act as a resistance level, as traders may be reluctant to buy above that price, while the bottom of a gap can act as a support level, as traders may be hesitant to sell below that price. These levels can influence future price movements and can be used by traders to make informed decisions.

Trading Opportunities: Gaps can provide trading opportunities for both short-term and long-term traders. For example, day traders may look to buy a stock that gaps up at the open and then sell it later in the day as the price continues to rise. Swing traders may look to buy a stock that gaps down and then hold it for several days or weeks, anticipating that the price will recover and fill the gap.

Market Sentiment: Gaps can also impact market sentiment. A gap up can indicate a bullish sentiment, as traders are willing to pay higher prices for the stock, while a gap down can indicate a bearish sentiment, as traders are willing to sell at lower prices. Market sentiment can influence the overall direction of the market and can be an important factor for traders to consider when making decisions.

How To Identify Gaps Visually On Charts

Identifying gaps on a stock chart is a straightforward process that involves visually inspecting the chart for sudden breaks or discontinuities in the price line or bars/candles, where no trading activity occurred between those price points. Here's how to spot different types of gaps on various chart types:

1. Line Charts

On a line chart, which connects the closing

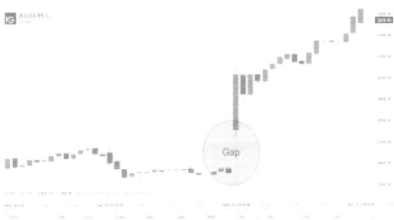

prices of stocks over time, a gap will appear as a sharp vertical break between two points on the line, with no gradual transition between them. Since line charts only plot closing prices, they might not capture all gaps, especially those filled within a trading day.

2. Bar and Candlestick Charts

Bar and candlestick charts provide a more detailed view, showing the open, high, low, and close prices for each period (day, hour, minute, etc.). Gaps are more easily spotted and understood in these charts:

- **Look for Empty Spaces:** On a bar or candlestick chart, a gap will appear as a space between two consecutive bars or candles, where the high of one period and the low of the next period (for a gap up) or the low of one period and the high of the next period (for a gap down) do not overlap.

- **Gap Up:** This occurs when the lowest price of the current period is higher than the highest price of the previous period. Visually, you'll see an upward gap on the chart.

- **Gap Down:** This happens when the highest price of the current period is lower than the lowest price of the previous period. The chart will show a downward gap.

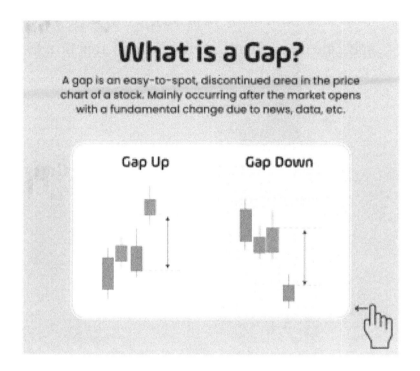

3. Volume

While not a direct method to identify the gap itself, looking at the trading volume can provide additional confirmation and significance to the gap. A gap accompanied by high volume is generally considered more significant and indicative of a stronger signal (whether bullish or bearish), as it suggests a substantial change in sentiment or reaction to the news.

How To Differentiate True Gaps From Wicks (False Gaps)

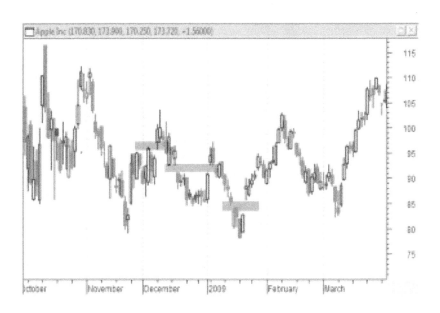

Differentiating between true gaps and wicks (false gaps) on a chart can be tricky at times, but here are some key points to help you:

True Gaps vs. Wicks (False Gaps):

- **True gaps:** These represent a genuine absence of trading activity between two periods. The price jumps significantly from one closing price to the next opening price, leaving a clear space on the chart.

- **Wicks (False gaps):** These are not true gaps but rather an illusion created by the way price bars or candlesticks are displayed. While the wick may appear to create a space, there was trading activity within that range, just not at the specific price level represented by the wick.

Here's how to distinguish them:

1. **Examine the price range:**

    o **True gaps:** The closing price of one period will not be within the range (high or low) of the next period's price bar.

    o **Wicks:** The closing price of one period will fall within the range (touch or be inside) of the next period's price bar, even if the wick itself extends beyond that range.

2. **Volume confirmation:**

    o **True gaps:** Often accompanied by **increased trading volume** on the day the gap forms, indicating significant buying or selling pressure.

- **Wicks:** May not necessarily have a significant increase in volume, as the trading activity happened within the main body of the price bar, not at the wick's level.

3. **Timeframe consideration:**

    - True gaps are more **independent of the timeframe** you're viewing the chart on. They will be present on all timeframes, as they represent a genuine discontinuity in price.

    - **Wicks can appear different on different timeframes:**

        - A wick on a shorter timeframe might appear like a true gap on a longer timeframe due to the lower level of detail displayed.

- Conversely, a wick on a longer timeframe might appear smaller or even disappear on a shorter timeframe due to the higher level of detail.

Additional Tips:

- Utilize **chart tools** that highlight gaps and wicks. Some software differentiates them visually with different colors or markings.

- Consider **combining visual identification with volume analysis** for a more robust assessment.

- **Focus on context:** Analyze gaps and wicks in their broader context, considering news events, technical indicators, and overall market trends, to improve your understanding of their potential significance.

Remember, differentiating gaps and wicks requires practice and should not be solely relied upon for trading decisions. Always consider the overall market context and conduct further analysis using other technical and fundamental factors before making any investment decisions.

Chapter 2: The different types of gaps Illustrated

Not all gaps are created equal. In the first chapter, we explored the fundamental concept of gaps in stock charts, those empty spaces that signal a jump in price between two trading periods. But just like fingerprints, each gap carries its own unique story, revealing valuable insights into the market's inner workings.

Some gaps are small and insignificant, while others are large and can signal major shifts in market sentiment. Some gaps are filled within a few trading days, while others remain unfilled for weeks or even months. Understanding the different types of gaps can provide valuable insights into the market and help you make more informed decisions.

In this chapter, we'll explore the various types of gaps that can occur in stock trading, including breakaway gaps, runaway gaps, exhaustion gaps, and common gaps. We'll examine how each type of gap forms, what they can indicate about market trends, and how you can use this information to your advantage.

Illustration Of The Different Types Of Gap

There are several types of gaps that can occur in stock trading, each with its unique characteristics and implications for market dynamics.

The primary types of gaps commonly identified and analyzed in stock trading

- Common gaps
- Breakaway gaps
- Continuation (or runaway) gaps
- Exhaustion gaps

- Island reversal gaps.

These categories cover the majority of gap scenarios encountered on the charts and provide traders with insights into market sentiment, trend strength, and potential reversals.

However, the categorization of gaps can sometimes extend beyond these basic types, incorporating more nuanced or specific scenarios depending on the analytical approach or the particular characteristics of the market movement.

Here's a list of the most common types of gaps:

- Earnings Gaps
- Breakout Gaps
- Gap Fill
- Gap and Go

- Gap Down
- Gap Up
- Full Gap
- Partial Gap
- Overnight Gap
- Intraday Gap
- Weekend Gap
- Holiday Gap
- Fading Gaps

How Gaps Are Classified

Gaps are classified based on their characteristics, the market context in which they occur, and their implications for future price movements. This classification helps traders and investors understand the potential impact of a gap on market sentiment and price direction. Here's a breakdown of how gaps are typically classified:

1. By Direction

- **Up Gaps (Gap Up):** When the low price of the current period is higher than the high price of the previous period. This indicates a bullish sentiment.

- **Down Gaps (Gap Down):** When the high price of the current period is lower than the low price of the previous period, indicating bearish sentiment.

2. By Location in Market Trend

- **Breakaway Gaps:** Occur at the end of a price pattern and signal the start of a new trend. They break away from the previous price range.

- **Continuation (or Runaway) Gaps:** Appear within a trend and suggest that the current trend will continue.

- **Exhaustion Gaps:** Found at the end of a trend, indicating that the current trend is running out of strength and may soon reverse.

- **Common Gaps:** Do not signify a market trend and can occur randomly in any market condition. They are often filled quickly.

3. By Trading Volume

- **High-Volume Gaps:** These gaps are accompanied by a significant increase in trading volume and are considered more significant for future price movements.

- **Low-Volume Gaps:** Occur with little change in trading volume and might be less significant, potentially indicating a temporary or less decisive market move.

4. By Context and Market Impact

- **Breakaway Gaps:** Signal the start of a new trend and a break from previous price patterns, often occurring with high volume.

- **Continuation or Runaway Gaps:** Indicate strong market sentiment in the direction of the current trend, usually seen with an increase in volume.

- **Exhaustion Gaps:** Suggest the end of a trend with a final push in price, often to be filled as the market reverses direction.

- **Common Gaps:** Frequently found in a trading range without indicating any significant market move, often filled quickly.

- **Island Reversal Gaps:** Feature a gap followed by a trading period (the "island") and then another gap in the opposite direction, signaling a potential reversal.

5. By Cause or Trigger

- **News Gaps:** Result from the immediate reaction to news, earnings reports, or other events that significantly impact the market's perception of a stock or asset.

- **Dividend Gaps:** Occur when the stock price adjusts for the dividend payout on the ex-dividend date.

Classifying gaps in these ways helps traders and analysts interpret the market's actions and make more informed decisions based on the likely implications of different types of gaps. Understanding the nature of a gap – its cause, context, and the market's response to it – is crucial for effectively incorporating gap analysis into a trading strategy.

Common Types of Gaps

Common gaps are like small breaks or jumps in the price of a stock that happen all the time. Imagine you're watching a movie, and suddenly there's a tiny skip where you miss a second or two of the action. In the stock market, this "skip" is where the price jumps up or down from one trade to the next, but it doesn't mean anything big is happening. It's just the normal ups and downs of trading.

These gaps are called "common" because they occur commonly and don't indicate any significant news or events affecting the stock. They are the market equivalent of taking a small step up or down on a staircase, rather than taking a giant leap. Often, these little gaps get filled pretty quickly, meaning the price moves back to where the gap started, just as if nothing happened.

Why Do Common Gaps Happen?

Common gaps can happen for a bunch of simple reasons, like small changes in supply and demand. Maybe a few more people want to sell than buy, so the price dips a little to find buyers, or vice versa.

Step-by-Step Guide to Identify a Common Gap on the Chart

Step 1: Choose Your Chart

- Start by opening a daily chart of the stock you're interested in. Common gaps can be seen in almost any timeframe, but daily charts are easy to work with.

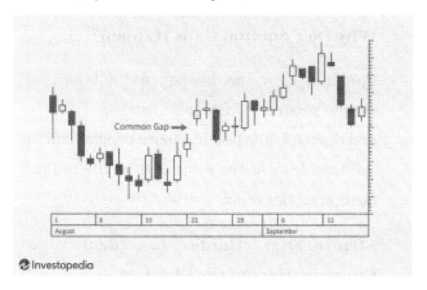

Step 2: Look for Small Jumps in Price

- Scan through the chart and look for places where the price jumps from one bar or candle to the next. Remember, you're looking for small jumps, not huge leaps.

Step 3: Check the Gap's Size

- A common gap usually isn't very big. It's just a small space between the close of one candle and the opening of the next. If the gap seems large, especially with increased volume, it might not be a common gap.

Step 4: Consider the Context

- See where the gap happened. If it's in the middle of a trading range and doesn't seem to be breaking out or making a new trend, it's likely a common gap. Common gaps don't signal any significant changes; they're just part of the stock's regular movement.

Step 5: Look for the Gap to Fill

- After identifying a potential common gap, watch it over the next few days. Many common gaps fill quickly, meaning the price will move back to cover the gap.

If it fills, you've likely spotted a common gap.

Step 6: Volume Check

- Though not always a rule, common gaps often don't have a significant increase in trading volume. If you see a gap with high volume, it might be another type of gap.

Break away Gaps

Breakaway gaps are significant price gaps on a stock chart that occur at the end of a price pattern, signaling the beginning of a new trend. These gaps indicate a strong shift in market sentiment away from the previous trading range or pattern.

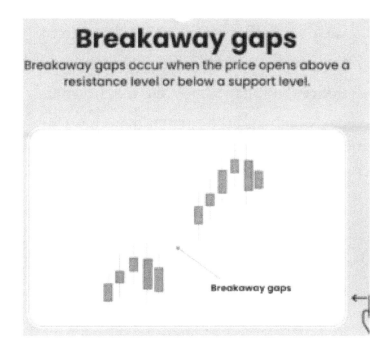

How to Identify Breakaway Gaps:

1. **Identify a Price Pattern:** First, look for a well-defined price pattern such as a trading range, consolidation pattern, or chart formation like a triangle or rectangle.

2. **Spot the Gap:** A breakaway gap occurs when the price breaks out of this pattern with a significant gap up or down from the previous trading range. You'll see a noticeable space between the previous day's high and the current day's low (for a gap up) or between the previous day's low and the current day's high (for a gap down).

3. **Confirm with Volume:** Breakaway gaps are typically accompanied by higher-than-average trading volume, indicating strong conviction from market participants in the direction of the gap.

4. **Check Trend Continuation:** Analyze the price action following the gap. If the price continues to move in the direction of the gap, it confirms the strength of the new trend initiated by the gap.

Why Breakaway Gaps Matter:

- Breakaway gaps provide traders with an early indication of a potential trend reversal or continuation.
- They offer opportunities for traders to enter positions early in a new trend, capturing potential profits as the trend develops.
- Breakaway gaps can serve as key levels of support or resistance in future price action, influencing trading decisions and risk management strategies.

In essence, breakaway gaps are like opening a new chapter in a stock's price story. They mark the beginning of a significant shift in market sentiment and provide traders with valuable insights into potential future price movements

Continuation gaps

Continuation gaps are significant price gaps on a stock chart that occur within an existing trend, signaling the likelihood of the current trend continuing. These gaps indicate a strong and sustained momentum in the direction of the prevailing trend.

How to Identify Continuation Gaps:

1. **Identify the Current Trend:** First, determine the direction of the prevailing trend by analyzing the stock's price action. This could be an uptrend (higher highs and higher lows) or a downtrend (lower highs and lower lows).

2. **Spot the Gap:** A continuation gap occurs when the price gaps are up (for an uptrend) or gaps down (for a downtrend) in the direction of the prevailing trend. You'll notice a gap between the previous day's close and the current day's open, indicating that the momentum of the trend is likely to persist.

3. **Confirm with Volume:** Continuation gaps are often accompanied by higher-than-average trading volume, reflecting strong participation from market participants aligned with the prevailing trend.

4. **Check Price Action Post-Gap:** Analyze how the price behaves after the gap. If the price continues to move in the direction of the trend, it confirms the strength of the existing trend and the validity of the continuation gap.

Exhaustion gaps

What are Exhaustion Gaps? Exhaustion gaps are significant price gaps on a stock chart that occur near the end of a trend, signaling the potential exhaustion of the prevailing trend's momentum. These gaps suggest that the market may be reaching a point of saturation, where the trend is losing strength and could be ripe for a reversal.

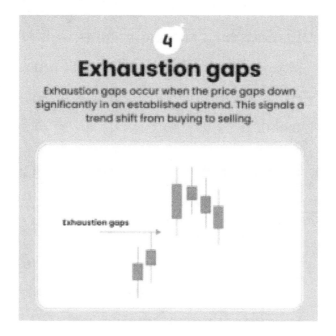

How to Identify Exhaustion Gaps:

1. **Identify the Current Trend:** Begin by identifying the prevailing trend in the stock's price action. This could be an uptrend or a downtrend.

2. **Spot the Gap:** An exhaustion gap occurs when the price gaps up (for an uptrend) or gaps down (for a downtrend) in the direction opposite to the prevailing trend. You'll observe a gap between the previous day's close and the current day's opening, indicating a sudden shift in sentiment.

3. **Confirm with Volume:** Exhaustion gaps may or may not be accompanied by significant trading volume. However, a decrease in volume relative to previous days can signal a loss of interest or conviction in the prevailing trend.

4. **Check Price Action Post-Gap:** Pay attention to how the price behaves after the gap. If the price fails to sustain the gap and starts moving in the opposite direction, it suggests that the trend may be losing steam and a reversal could be imminent.

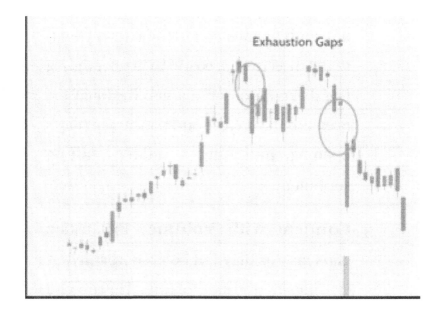

Example Scenario: Imagine a stock has been in a prolonged uptrend, making higher highs and higher lows. As the uptrend progresses, the stock experiences an exhaustion gap where it gaps up from $90 to $95. However, instead of continuing higher, the price quickly reverses course and starts to decline. This gap signals that buyers may be exhausted, and the uptrend could be coming to an end.

Why Exhaustion Gaps Matter:

- Exhaustion gaps provide early warnings of potential trend reversals, allowing traders to prepare for a change in market sentiment.

- They offer opportunities for traders to consider taking profits on existing positions or even initiating new positions in anticipation of a trend reversal.

- Exhaustion gaps can serve as significant price levels in future price action, acting as resistance (for uptrends) or support (for downtrends) as the market reacts to the exhaustion of the previous trend.

In essence, exhaustion gaps act as a cautionary signal, indicating that the prevailing trend may be running out of steam. By recognizing and interpreting these gaps, traders can position themselves strategically for potential trend reversals and capitalize on new trading opportunities.

Runaway Gap

Runaway gaps, also known as continuation gaps, are significant price gaps on a stock chart that occur within an existing trend, signaling the likelihood of the current trend continuing with renewed momentum. These gaps indicate strong and sustained market sentiment in the direction of the prevailing trend.

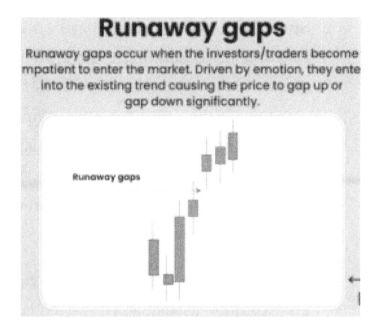

How to Identify Runaway Gaps:

1. **Identify the Current Trend:** Begin by identifying the direction of the prevailing trend in the stock's price action. This could be an uptrend (higher highs and higher lows) or a downtrend (lower highs and lower lows).

2. **Spot the Gap:** A runaway gap occurs when the price gaps up (for an uptrend) or gaps down (for a downtrend) in the direction of the prevailing trend. You'll observe a gap between the previous day's close and the current day's open, indicating a continuation of the trend with increased momentum.

3. **Confirm with Volume:** Runaway gaps are typically accompanied by higher-than-average trading volume, reflecting strong participation from market participants aligned with the prevailing trend.

4. **Check Price Action Post-Gap:** Pay attention to how the price behaves after the gap. If the price continues to move strongly in the direction of the trend, it confirms the strength and validity of the runaway gap.

Example Scenario: Imagine a stock has been trending upwards, making higher highs

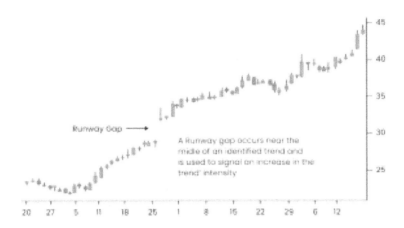

and higher lows. During this uptrend, the stock experiences a runaway gap where it gaps up from $70 to $75 on above-average volume. This gap suggests that the bullish momentum is likely to persist, and the uptrend may continue with renewed vigor.

Why Runaway Gaps Matter:

- Runaway gaps provide traders with confirmation of the prevailing trend's strength and momentum.

- They offer opportunities for traders to add to existing positions or enter new positions in the direction of the trend, potentially capturing further profits.

- Runaway gaps can serve as support or resistance levels in future price action, guiding trading decisions and risk management strategies.

In essence, runaway gaps act as accelerators of the current trend, indicating a surge in market sentiment and momentum. By recognizing and interpreting these gaps, traders can ride the wave of the prevailing trend and capitalize on potential trading opportunities.

Chapter 3: Gap Trading Strategies

Gap and Go

The "Gap and Go" trading strategy is a popular and dynamic approach used by day traders to capitalize on stocks that make a significant gap up or down at the market open, with the expectation that the price will continue in the direction of the gap throughout the trading day. This strategy is predicated on momentum and volume, indicating strong buyer or seller interest

In our recorded webinar I discuss the Stock Trading Strategy that I use every single day. My focus each day is the same. Finding the big gappers, hunting for the catalyst, creating a watchlist, and executing my trades according to the strategy.

This is the same thing every day. Repetition is what makes us so good at these strategies. Discipline is what keeps us profitable. Learning a Strategy for Day Trading the "Gaps" or "Gappers" is critical for success in the market!

I trade a Gap and Go! Stock Trading Strategy. Every day I start the same way. I look at the gappers that are more than 4% using my pre-market scanning tools from Trade-Ideas.

Gaps of more than 4% are good for Gap and Go! trading, Gaps of less than 4% are usually going to be filled but I don't find them as interesting. Once I have found the stocks already moving I search for a catalyst. I use StockTwits, Market Watch, and Benzinga to hunt for news.

Only after confirming the catalyst I will begin to look for an entry. My Gap and Go! The strategy is very similar to my Momentum Day Trading Strategy. The difference is that the

Gap and Go! The strategy is specifically for trades between 9:30-10 am.

I look for quick and easy trades right as the market opens. Gap and Go! is a quick stock trading strategy to give us a profit usually by 10 am.

Gapper Checklist

1) Scan for all gappers more than 4%
2) Hunt for Catalyst for the gap (earnings, news, PR, etc)
3) Mark out pre-market highs and highs of any pre-market flags
4) Prepare an order to buy the pre-market highs once the market opens
5) At 9:30 am as soon as the bell rings I buy the high of the first 1min candle (1min opening range breakout) with a stop at the low of that candle or buy the Pre-Market highs.

Gap and Go Entry Setups

1) Break of Pre-market flags
2) Opening Range Breakouts
3) Red to Green Moves

Entry Setups 4. 5. and 6. are for Trading Course Students Only.

The Importance of Float

Always look for low-float. These will have home run potential written all over them. A stock that has a 10mil share float and trades 1mil share pre-market has already traded 10% of the float.

There is an extremely good chance the entire float will be traded during the day once the market is open. These are the type of stocks that can run 50-100% in one day.

When we have the right catalyst, float, and retail trader interest, it's the perfect storm for a big   runner.

Review of Stock Trading Strategy "Gap and Go!" Scanner Results

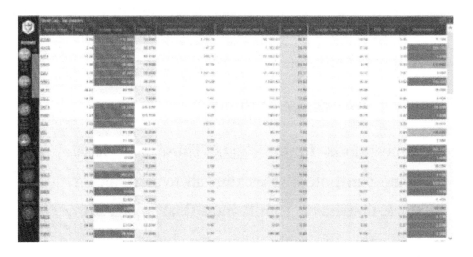

Why do Prices GAP up?

- Gaps Greatest imbalance between demand and supply. The gap is up because of the aggressiveness of buyers. I mean, there are more buy orders at the open than there is available supply at the prior day's closing price. The gap is down because of the aggressiveness of the sellers. There are more sell orders at the open than willing demand at the prior day's close. Therefore, gaps are almost always at price levels with a supply and demand imbalance at the open.

- Gaps also occur due to the participant's overnight sentiment or big news.

- Smart money is trying to skip important support and resistance levels, i.e., If they are bullish, they GAP up price above the supply zone.

GAP acts as Support and Resistance

The Up gap acts as a support zone, and the down gap acts as a resistance zone. The chart below of RELIANCE stock shows the GAP up acting as support for prices.

The Gap fill

The gap-fill refers to the price retrace and close the level where the origin of the gap occurs. The closure rate (gap-fill) for up gaps increases if the prior day's open-to-close price trend increases. The closure rate (gap-fill) for down gaps increases if the prior day's open-to-close move is downward.

After the GAP, the price tries to fill the gap. Another occurrence with gaps is that once holes are filled by price, the gap tends to reverse direction and continue in the direction of the gap (for example, in the chart BELOW of RELIANCE, back upwards).

Types of Gap Trading Strategy

Gaps are divided based on the context in which they appear.

1. Breakaway (or Breakout) Gaps

2. Runaway (or Measuring) Gaps

3. Exhaustion Gaps

4. Professional gap

5. Inside gap

What is the breakaway GAP?

The breakaway gap means breaking the important support or resistance or significant trend line in the form of the gap. Generally appears after completion of important patterns like price in consolidation range or any continuation or reversal pattern. In maximum time, this gap does not fill quickly or on the same day. The most important volume should be high.

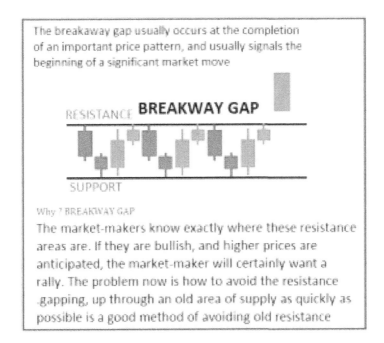

Why does the breakaway gap occur?

The smart money knows exactly where these resistance areas are. If the smart money is bullish and higher prices are anticipated, the smart money will certainly want a rally. The problem now is how to avoid the old resistance.

- Gapping up through an old supply area as quickly as possible is an old and trusted method – avoiding resistance.

We now have a clear sign of strength. Smart money does not want to have to buy the stock at high prices. They have already bought their main holding at lower levels.

Smart money knows that a breakout above an old trading resistance area will create a new wave of buying. How?

- Many traders who have shorted the market will now be forced to cover their poor positions by buying.

- Many traders are looking for breakouts to buy.

- All those traders who are not in the market may feel they are missing out and will be encouraged to start buying.

Here, you can see that prices have been quickly moved by smart money, whose opinion of the market is bullish. We know this because the volume has *increased*. It cannot be a trap-up move because the high volume supports the move.

The chart study above shows breakaway gaps through important support and resistance levels. Every breakaway gap leads to a trend continuation as well.

Runaway (or Measuring) Gap:

After the move has been underway for a while, prices will GAP somewhere around the middle of the move. This gap is called the runaway gap.

In an uptrend, it is a sign of continuation of a trend; in a downtrend, it is a sign of continuation of the trend.

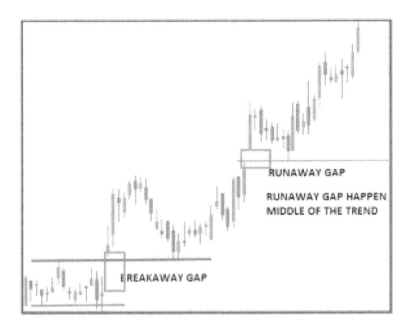

Exhaustion Gap:

You will find that weak gap-ups are always Gap up to resistance or gap down to support. This price action is usually designed to trap you into a potentially weak market and a poor trade, catching stop-losses on the short side and generally panicking traders to do the wrong thing.

Near the end of an uptrend, the exhaustion gap occurred. However, that upward gap quickly fades, and prices turn lower. When prices close under that last gap (exhaustion gap), it is usually a dead giveaway that the exhaustion gap has appeared. An exhaustion gap occurs with extremely high volume.

Professional GAP Trading Strategy

These gaps appear at the beginning of the moves. Generally, it occurs in the supply or demand zone. (Gap up from demand zone and gap down from supply zone) when price approaches the quality supply and demand zone

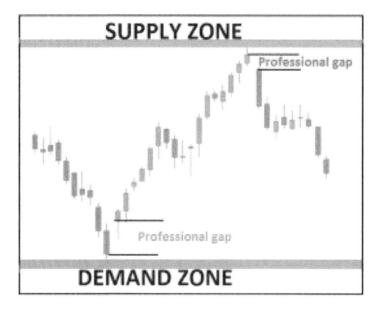

Inside GAP Trading Strategy

Inside gaps are gaps happening inside the prior day's range.

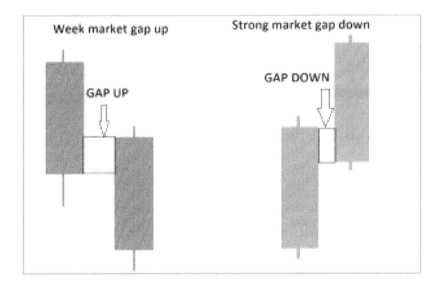

1. Week market gap up
2. Strong market gap down

However, low volume warns you of a trap up-move (which is indicative of a lack of demand in the market) after a gap up resistance

Gap Trading Strategy:

There are three factors to monitor to determine whether the gap is real or trapped. The three factors are volume, opening price, and pullback

Opening Price and Pullback

After a gap up, the pullback to be watched

- Flat pullback (price consolidates high of the day). Strong buy signal

- The weak pullback was unable to close below the previous day's high. buy signal

- Strong pullback closes below the previous day's high. sell signal

If the stock gaps up and then sells off and remains beneath its opening price after the morning pullback has stabilized, the stock may have reached its high of the day. however, if a stock gaps up and pulls back during the morning pullback but then rallies to break above its opening price, the mark-up was probably not trapped GAP, and the stock should make new intraday highs

Volume

- It is important to watch the volume carefully when determining if a gap is valid. If the stock GAPs up high, the volume is also high, and the price remains above its opening price after the early morning pullback, it is an excellent sign that the stock has further to go on the upside. All reverse for a trap gap up

- If high volume appears after a gap up and the stock immediately comes under selling pressure, chances are that this volume was a seller.

- If a large volume of paper a gap up the situation and the stock runs higher, then chances are that it was a buyer, probably the reason for the gap up in the first place. The smart money will support the stock if he has the buyer, or he will sell stock quickly if he has the sellers. Smart money does not generally chase the stock in the direction of the gap in the early morning unless there is a fundamental reason for doing so

Our entry is based on two types of gap

1. Outside gap(market open outside of the previous day range)
2. Inside gap(market open inside of the previous day range)

Outside gap

1. Gap and GO Trading Strategy

All gaps are not filled in that day

Gap and GO Trading Strategy criteria

1. The price GAP up above the previous day's high

2. Wait for the first candle to complete

3. Volume should be high and supporting in the direction of the gap

4. Mark opening range

5. Entry on breakout of high of the day

6. The price should be above VWAP.

Peter L. Mcgrew

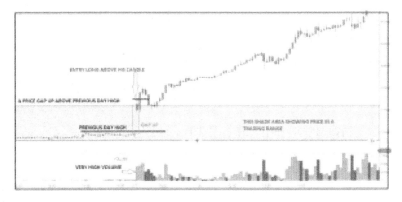

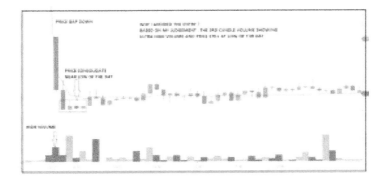

2. Gap-fill reversal Trading Strategy

When a market gaps up, then the gap acts as a support level for any pullback. Pullback Tests of gaps on lighter volume tell that the issue does not have enough energy to get through the gap; instead, the gap becomes support, and our buy entry triggers any bullish signal

1. Wait for the price gap to go up

2. Please wait for a stock to pull back to its prior day's close and fill the gap.

Two types of Pullback

1. The price gap is up just above the previous day's high or below the previous day's low, and then a strong pin bar is formed, which fills the gap. volume should be high on the pin bar.

2. The second price gap is up, and then retrace and fill the gap. it takes more than 2 candles, and the volume should be decreasing.

3. You then wait to see a sign of strength and enter the position on that move.

4. Price should not close inside the previous day in any five-minute candle.

5. You then place a stop below the low of the candlestick.

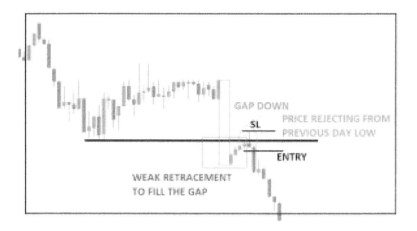

3. Open Gap Reversal Trading Strategy

These patterns generally appear at the top or bottom or in any strong supply or demand zone.

The open gap reversal process

1. The chart needs an extended uptrend for at least a few trading sessions to the supply zone. A gap up in price to quality supply zone is a VERY high odds shorting opportunity.

2. Or a GAP up in price to quality supply zone in a downtrend is a VERY high odds shorting opportunity.

3. After a GAP up, the price started falling and crosses yesterday. This generates the sale.

4. The Stop-Loss is the low of the same day.

NOTE:-As we are trading against the gap, more confirmation is required confirmation, either from price action or volume action

Peter L. Mcgrew

4 & 5. Inside GAP Trading Strategy

Let's analyze a downtrend, and the previous day was a downday. Today's price gap is up but close to the previous day's range. Our entry opportunity will be

- Gap up short
- Gap up long

In the context of a downtrend, a gap up in price is a VERY high odds shorting opportunity if any bearish reversal signal is given. A gap up in price, in the context of a downtrend, is a lower odds buying opportunity.

If the stock gaps up and then sells off and remains beneath its opening price after the morning pullback has stabilized, the stock may have reached its high of the day. however, if a stock gaps up and pulls back during the morning pullback but then rallies to break above its opening price, the mark-up was probably not trapped gap, and the stock should make new intraday highs

In an uptrend, entry opportunities will be

1. Gap down long
2. Gap down short

Gap up short in a downtrend

- Context downtrend
- Wait for at least 5 minutes. Or mark the opening range
- After the 5 minutes, wait for a reversal price signal to provide short-term confirmation that the markup was a trap by smart money and the short-term trend is pointing downward.
- The short below the first candle

- Volume should be below. If the stock has a GAP up high, the volume should be high to confirm the real gap. However, if the price closes below the opening price with no large volume, chances are that the mark-up was a trap by smart money.

Let's analyze the gap down long in an uptrend

Gap up long in a downtrend

How to know whether the gap up is real or trapped by smart money

- When the gap opens, the volume should be heavy to go higher. if smart money is actively supported by volume

- Wait and see if the market trades above its opening prices after the morning pullback. It indicates the gap was real

- Then go along

- Or you can enter from a previous day's low when the price retrace test of the previous day's low.

Note: – This entry technique is very risky as we are going against the trend and momentum, so double confirmation is required

Combining our Pullback Trading Strategy and the Advance CANDLESTICK Analysis article is very useful for this trading strategy.

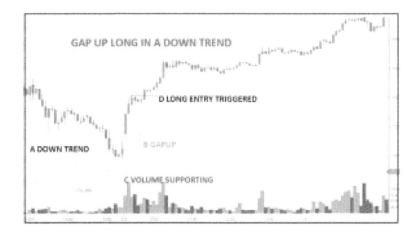

Gap Trading Strategies Summary:

Gap trading strategies revolve around the principle that price movements will eventually fill the gap. A "gap" in trading refers to a sharp break between prices on a chart where no trading occurs, resulting in a visible discontinuity. This typically occurs between the close of the market on one day and its opening on the next. Gaps are often caused by economic data, earnings reports, or other significant news events that occur when the markets are closed.

Types of Gaps

- **Common Gaps:** These occur without any major news or events and are typically filled quickly.

- **Breakaway Gaps:** Occur at the end of a price pattern and signal the beginning of a new trend.

- **Runaway Gaps:** Also known as continuation gaps, occur in the middle of a trend and signal its continuation.

- **Exhaustion Gaps:** Occur near the end of a price pattern and signal a final attempt to hit new highs or lows.

Gap Trading Strategies:

- **Gap and Go Strategy:** This involves identifying stocks with significant gaps at the market opening and trading toward the gap. Traders look for high volume and significant news to validate the gap.

- **Gap Fill Strategy:** This strategy is based on the observation that prices often "fill" the gap. A trader would buy or sell, expecting the price to return to its previous level.

- **Breakaway Gap Trading:** When a gap occurs with strong volume and after a period of consolidation, it may indicate the start of a new trend. Traders might enter a position in the direction of the gap.

- **Runaway Gap Trading:** In a strong trend, a gap can indicate further movement in the direction of the trend. Traders might use these gaps to add to their positions.

- **Exhaustion Gap Trading:** These are identified towards the end of a trend and might signal a reversal. Traders might look for low volume and other indicators to confirm.

When using gap trading strategies, here are some important considerations:

- **Volume:** A high volume after a gap is generally seen as a confirmation that the gap will not be filled immediately and that the new price represents a new consensus on value.

- **Context:** The underlying reason for the gap should be considered. For instance, a gap caused by a major fundamental shift in the company's outlook (like a merger or an acquisition) is less likely to be filled than a gap caused by short-term factors.

- **Time Frame:** Some traders look for gaps on daily charts, while others look for intraday gaps within the trading day.

- **Risk Management:** Using stop-loss orders when gap trading is critical because the price can move quickly and unexpectedly after a gap.

Limitations and Risks of GAP Trading Strategies

- **False Signals:** Not all gaps lead to predictable outcomes. Sometimes, gaps don't get filled as expected, or the trend doesn't continue as projected.

- **Market Volatility:** Gaps often occur in volatile market conditions, increasing the risk of trading.

- **Overnight Risk:** In some cases, holding a position overnight to capitalize on or wait for a gap to fill can be risky, especially if unpredictable events occur.

Chapter 4: Risk management for trading gaps

Gap trading, a strategy that capitalizes on price discrepancies between the close of one trading session and the open of the next, offers lucrative opportunities for traders. However, navigating the volatility and unpredictability inherent in gap trading requires a solid foundation in risk management. This chapter delves into the critical importance of risk management in gap trading and provides practical strategies to mitigate potential losses while maximizing profit potential.

Gap trading presents unique challenges and opportunities due to the sudden and often significant price movements that occur during market gaps. Whether caused by earnings reports, news events, or other factors, these gaps can provide traders with ample opportunities for profit, but they also carry inherent risks.

Effective risk management is paramount in mitigating these risks and ensuring long-term success in gap trading. By implementing sound risk management principles, traders can protect their capital, maintain consistency in their trading approach, and navigate the psychological challenges that arise in volatile market conditions.

Throughout this chapter, we will explore various aspects of risk management in gap trading, including setting stop loss orders, determining position sizes, diversification techniques, managing emotions, and reviewing past trades. By understanding and implementing these strategies, traders can enhance their ability to capitalize on gap trading opportunities while minimizing potential losses.

Market Volatility and Gap Trading:

Market volatility plays a pivotal role in gap trading, as it often contributes to the occurrence and magnitude of price gaps. Traders must recognize that heightened volatility can increase the likelihood of larger and more frequent gaps, amplifying both profit potential and risk. While volatility can present lucrative trading opportunities, it also demands a heightened focus on risk management.

1. Impact of Volatility: Understanding how volatility influences gap formation is crucial. High volatility tends to precede significant market movements, leading to larger price gaps. Traders must assess

current market volatility levels and adjust their risk management strategies accordingly.

2. Adjusting Strategies: During periods of heightened volatility, traders may opt to reduce position sizes or widen stop loss orders to account for increased price fluctuations. Additionally, implementing volatility-based indicators or metrics can aid in gauging market conditions and adjusting trading strategies accordingly.

B. Potential Impact of Gaps on Positions:

Gap trading introduces a unique set of risks that can significantly impact trading positions. Traders must carefully assess the potential consequences of price gaps on their existing positions and develop proactive risk management strategies to mitigate adverse outcomes.

1. Price Dislocation: Gaps can result in price dislocation, where the opening price significantly deviates from the previous closing price. This can lead to sudden losses or gains for traders with existing positions, depending on the direction of the gap and their market exposure.

2. Slippage: Gap trading may also expose traders to slippage, where orders are executed at prices different from the expected entry or exit levels. Slippage can occur due to the rapid price movement associated with gaps, resulting in unexpected losses or reduced profitability.

C. Historical Analysis of Gap Behavior:

Conducting a historical analysis of gap behavior can provide valuable insights into the frequency, magnitude, and direction of price gaps within specific markets or instruments. By examining past gap occurrences, traders can better anticipate future gap behavior and develop informed risk management strategies.

1. Data Collection: Traders can collect historical price data and identify instances of price gaps within their chosen markets or instruments. This data should include gap size, direction, and any relevant market conditions surrounding the gap event.

2. Pattern Recognition: Analyzing historical gap data allows traders to identify recurring patterns or trends in gap behavior. By recognizing common characteristics of past gaps, traders can anticipate potential gap scenarios and adjust their risk management strategies accordingly.

Understanding the risks associated with gap trading, including market volatility, the potential impact of gaps on positions, and historical gap behavior, is essential for effective risk management. By acknowledging these risks and implementing proactive risk management strategies, traders can navigate the challenges of gap trading with confidence and resilience.

Position sizing analysis

A. Calculating Position Size Based on Gap Risk:

1. Determine Risk Tolerance: Before calculating position size based on gap risk, traders must first establish their risk tolerance. This involves determining the maximum acceptable loss per trade as a percentage of the trading capital.

2. Assess Gap Risk: Evaluate the size and direction of the gap to assess its potential impact on the trading position. Consider factors such as the gap magnitude, market conditions, and the trader's analysis of the gap's significance.

3. Set Stop Loss Level: Determine the appropriate stop loss level based on the gap's risk profile and the trader's risk tolerance. The stop loss level should be positioned to limit potential losses to the predetermined risk threshold.

4. Calculate Position Size: Use the formula for position sizing to calculate the appropriate position size based on the gap risk and the predetermined stop loss level. The formula typically involves dividing the maximum acceptable loss per trade by the difference between the entry price and the stop loss level.

5. Adjust for Leverage and Margin: If trading with leverage or margin, consider the impact of leverage on position size and margin requirements. Ensure that the position size is adjusted accordingly to account for leverage and margin constraints.

6. Review and Confirm: Double-check the calculated position size to ensure accuracy and alignment with risk management objectives. Confirm that the position size reflects the desired risk-reward profile and is consistent with the trader's overall trading strategy.

B. Using Volatility Metrics for Position Sizing:

1. Measure Market Volatility: Utilize volatility metrics such as average true range (ATR) or standard deviation to gauge market volatility levels. These

metrics provide insights into the average price range or variability of the market over a specific period.

2. Determine Volatility-Based Position Size: Adjust position size based on the current level of market volatility. Higher volatility may warrant smaller position sizes to account for increased price fluctuations and potential risk.

3. Set Volatility-Based Stop Loss: Calculate stop loss levels based on volatility metrics to account for potential price movements. Adjust stop loss distances to reflect the prevailing market volatility and ensure adequate protection against adverse price fluctuations.

4. Implement Dynamic Position Sizing: Consider implementing dynamic position sizing strategies that adapt to

changes in market volatility. Adjust position sizes periodically based on evolving market conditions to maintain alignment with risk management objectives.

C. Balancing Risk-Reward Ratios in Gap Trading:

1. Define Risk-Reward Ratio: Determine the desired risk-reward ratio for gap trades, specifying the ratio of potential reward to potential risk. Common risk-reward ratios include 1:1, 2:1, or 3:1, where the potential reward is a multiple of the potential risk.

2. Assess Profit Targets: Identify potential profit targets based on technical analysis, support and resistance levels, or other relevant factors. Ensure that profit targets align with the desired risk-reward

ratio and provide adequate reward potential relative to the risk taken.

3. **Adjust Position Size Accordingly:** Calculate position sizes that allow for the desired risk-reward ratio based on the predetermined stop loss and profit target levels. Ensure that the potential reward justifies the risk undertaken and maintains a balanced risk-reward profile.

4. **Monitor and Adjust:** Continuously monitor gap trades and assess their progress relative to the defined risk-reward ratio. If necessary, adjust stop loss and profit target levels to maintain alignment with risk management objectives and optimize risk-adjusted returns.

Emotion Management

A. Psychology of Gap Trading:

1. Understand Market Psychology: Recognize the psychological factors that influence gap trading, including fear, greed, and market sentiment. Understand that price gaps often trigger emotional responses in traders, leading to impulsive decision-making.

2. Acknowledge Behavioral Biases: Be aware of common behavioral biases such as confirmation bias, overconfidence, and loss aversion that can impact decision-making during gap trading. Recognize how these biases can cloud judgment and lead to irrational trading decisions.

3. Control Emotional Responses: Develop emotional intelligence and mindfulness techniques to manage emotional responses during gap trading. Practice self-awareness and recognize when emotions are influencing trading decisions, then take steps to regain emotional balance.

4. Focus on Process Over Outcome: Shift focus from short-term outcomes to the trading process itself. Emphasize disciplined execution of trading strategies and risk management principles rather than fixating on individual trade outcomes.

B. Controlling Fear and Greed:

1. Identify Triggers: Recognize the triggers that evoke fear and greed during gap trading, such as large price movements,

unexpected news events, or perceived missed opportunities. Identify specific scenarios or situations that tend to amplify emotional responses.

2. Establish Trading Rules: Develop a set of trading rules and guidelines that help mitigate fear and greed. Set predefined entry and exit criteria, stop loss levels, and profit targets based on objective analysis rather than emotional impulses.

3. Implement Risk Management: Prioritize risk management strategies to mitigate fear of losses. Set appropriate stop loss orders and position sizes based on risk tolerance and market conditions to limit potential downside risk.

4. Practice Patience and Discipline: Cultivate patience and discipline in decision-making processes. Avoid

impulsive actions driven by fear of missing out (FOMO) or the desire to recoup losses quickly. Stick to trading plans and avoid chasing after emotionally charged trades.

C. Techniques for Staying Disciplined During Gap Trading:

1. Develop a Trading Plan: Create a comprehensive trading plan that outlines entry and exit strategies, risk management rules, and trading objectives. Refer to the trading plan consistently and adhere to its guidelines during gap trading.

2. Maintain Trading Journal: Keep a detailed trading journal to document trade entries, exits, and outcomes. Reviewing past trades helps reinforce discipline and accountability while

providing insights into trading performance and areas for improvement.

3. Set Realistic Expectations: Manage expectations by setting realistic goals and objectives for gap trading. Recognize that consistent profitability takes time and effort, and avoid succumbing to unrealistic expectations or the allure of get-rich-quick schemes.

4. Utilize Visualization Techniques: Use visualization techniques to mentally rehearse trading scenarios and practice maintaining discipline under pressure. Visualize yourself calmly executing trading strategies and adhering to risk management principles during volatile market conditions.

Backtesting and Review

A. Importance of Backtesting Gap Trading Strategies:

1. Understand Strategy Effectiveness: Backtesting allows traders to assess the effectiveness of their gap trading strategies by simulating trades using historical data. By backtesting various strategies, traders can determine which approaches are likely to yield favorable results in different market conditions.

2. Validate Risk Management: Backtesting helps validate risk management techniques and assess their impact on overall trading performance. Traders can evaluate the efficacy of stop-loss orders, position-sizing strategies, and other risk

management principles in limiting losses and maximizing profitability.

3. Identify Strengths and Weaknesses: Through backtesting, traders can identify the strengths and weaknesses of their gap trading strategies. By analyzing historical performance data, traders can pinpoint areas of improvement and refine their approaches to better align with market dynamics.

4. Build Confidence: Successful backtesting results can instill confidence in traders by demonstrating the robustness of their trading strategies. Confidence in one's approach can help traders maintain discipline during live trading and avoid emotional decision-making.

B. Analyzing Gap Trading Performance:

1. Evaluate Trade Outcomes: Analyze the outcomes of gap trades based on predetermined criteria, including profitability, risk-reward ratios, and win-loss ratios. Assess whether trades align with the intended trading strategy and risk management principles.

2. Review Trade Execution: Evaluate the execution of gap trades to identify any discrepancies between planned and actual entry and exit points. Assess whether trades were executed in accordance with the trading plan and whether any deviations occurred.

3. Measure Performance Metrics: Calculate key performance metrics such as average return per trade, maximum drawdown, and Sharpe ratio to assess overall trading performance. Compare performance

metrics to benchmarks or industry standards to gauge relative success.

4. Identify Patterns and Trends: Look for patterns and trends in gap trading performance, including recurring successes or failures, correlations with market conditions, and evolving performance over time. Identify any patterns that may indicate areas for improvement or adjustment.

C. Learning from Past Trades and Adjusting Strategies:

1. Review Trade Logs: Maintain detailed records of gap trades in a trade log or journal, documenting entry and exit points, trade rationale, and outcomes. Review trade logs regularly to identify patterns, trends, and areas for improvement.

2. Identify Learning Opportunities: Reflect on past trades to identify learning opportunities and lessons learned. Analyze both successful and unsuccessful trades to understand what contributed to each outcome and how to replicate or avoid similar situations in the future.

3. Adjust Trading Strategies: Based on insights gained from backtesting and trade analysis, make adjustments to gap trading strategies as needed. Modify entry and exit criteria, refine risk management techniques, or explore new approaches based on observed patterns and trends.

4. Continuously Improve: Embrace a mindset of continuous improvement and adaptation in gap trading. Regularly revisit and refine trading strategies based on new insights, market developments,

and evolving trading objectives. Remain open to experimentation and innovation to stay ahead in the dynamic market environment.

So, dear traders, as we wrap up our exploration of gap trading, let's take a moment to reflect on the key strategies we've discussed and the exciting opportunities that lie ahead.

Firstly, remember the importance of continuous learning and adaptation. The world of trading is ever-evolving, and staying ahead means staying informed. Keep exploring new techniques, analyzing market trends, and seeking out educational resources. Embrace every opportunity to expand your knowledge and refine your skills.

And let's not forget the power of encouragement. Disciplined and informed gap trading practices can lead to remarkable success. So, stay disciplined in your approach, stick to your trading plan, and trust in your abilities. Remember, every trade is a learning experience, and every setback is an opportunity to grow stronger.

So, as you embark on your gap trading journey, do so with confidence, enthusiasm, and a commitment to continuous improvement. Embrace the challenges, celebrate the victories, and never stop striving for greatness.

Happy trading, and may the gaps be ever in your favor!